30 Minute or Less Power Pressure Cooker XL Cookbook

Quick, Simple and Healthy Power Pressure Cooker Recipes

Danielle Jones

Warning-Disclaimer

The purpose of this book is to educate and entertain. The author or publisher does not guarantee that anyone following the techniques, suggestions, tips, ideas, or strategies will become successful. The author and publisher shall have neither liability or responsibility to anyone with respect to any loss or damage caused, or alleged to be caused, directly or indirectly by the information contained in this book.

TABLE OF CONTENTS

Introduction 7

Power Pressure Cooker XL: The Revolutionary Cooking Appliance... 8

Breakfast Recipes 14

Cheesy Eggs and Arugula in Hollandaise Sauce 14

Cheese and Thyme Cremini Oats...15

Crustless Three-Meat Quiche 16

Breakfast Vanilla Quinoa Bowl 17

Crispy Bacon and Egg Sandwich 17

Zesty and Citrusy French Toast 18

Cheddar, Ham, and Eggs Hash Bake 19

Giant Coconut Pancake...20

Sweet Potato, Tomato, and Onion Frittata.................................21

Cherry and Chocolate Oatmeal 22

Chorizo and Kale Egg Casserole...22

Banana and Cinnamon French Toast 23

Soups and Stews 25

Ham and Pea Soup..25

Tortellini Minestrone Soup...26

Mushroom and Beef Stew..27

Chicken Enchilada Soup...28

Lentil Soup 29

Irish Lamb Stew...30

Navy Bean and Ham Shank Soup 31

kSkim and Fast Miso and Tofu Soup 32

Pomodoro Soup 33

Pressure Cooked Chili..34

Pumpkin, Corn, and Chicken Chowder 35

Spicy Beef and Potato Soup...36

Creamy Curried Cauliflower Soup 37

Poultry Recipes 38

Hot and Spicy Shredded Chicken...38

Teriyaki Chicken Under Pressure...39

Creamy Turkey and Mushrooms..40

Simple Pressure Cooked Whole Chicken...41

Turkey and Potatoes in Buffalo Sauce 42

Fall-Off-Bone Drumsticks 42

Chicken Piccata.. 43

Salsa and Lime Chicken with Rice 44

Creamy and Garlicky Italian Spinach Chicken 45

Cherry Tomato, Olive, and Basil Chicken Casserole 46

Red Meat Recipes 48

Lamb Shanks Braised Under Pressure 48

Sticky Baby Back Ribs 49

Saucy Beef Tips and Rice 50

Worcestershire Pork Chops 51

Potted Rump Steak..52

Sloppy Joes and Coleslaw...53

Pot Roast in Peach Sauce...54

Shredded Beef the Caribbean Way 55

Smokey Pork Roast..56

Beef with Cabbage, Potatoes, and Carrots 57

Beef and Cheese Taco Pie 58

Herbed Lamb Roast with Potatoes 59

Seafood Recipes 60

Clams in White Wine 60

Almond-Crusted Tilapia.. 61

Shrimp and Egg Risotto 62

Lobster and Gruyere Pasta 63

Mediterranean Salmon 64

Tuna and Pea Cheesy Noodles..64

Scallops and Mussels Cauliflower Paella 65

Wrapped Fish and Potatoes 66

Lemon Sauce Salmon..67

Creamy Crabmeat.. 68

Cod in a Tomato Sauce 69

Vegetarian Recipes 70

Meatless Shepherd's Pie 70

Vegetarian Spaghetti Bolognese..71

Pressure Cooked Ratatouille 72

Bean and Rice Casserole..73

Potato Chili 73

Veggie Burger Patties 74

Fake Mushroom Risotto the Paleo Way 75

Spicy Moong Beans 76

Tamari Tofu with Sweet Potatoes and Broccoli............................77

Tomato Zoodles 78

Sweet Potato and Baby Carrot Medley..79

Leafy Green Risotto 80

Appetizers Recipes 82

Thyme-Flavored Fries 82

Buttery Parsley Corn 82

Kale Chips with Garlic and Lime Juice 83

Creamy Potato Slices with Chives 84

Hummus Under Pressure 85

Barbecue Wings 86

Mini Mac and Cheese 86

Asparagus Dressed in Bacon 87

Lemony and Garlicky Potato and Turnip Dip 88

Pressure Cooked Devilled Eggs 88

Easy Street Sweet Corn 89

Dessert Recipes **90**

Full Coconut Cake 90

Compote with Blueberries and Lemon Juice 91

Oatmeal Chocolate Cookies 91

Peanut Butter Bars 92

Poached Pears with Orange and Ginger 93

Milk Dumplings in Sweet Cardamom Sauce 94

Pressure Cooked Cherry Pie 95

Crème Caramel Coconut Flan 96

Lemon and Chocolate Bread Pudding 97

Easiest Pressure Cooked Raspberry Curd 98

A Different Pumpkin Pie 99

Conclusion **100**

INTRODUCTION

Pressure cookers offer an efficient, time-saving, and absolutely effortless way to enjoy a delicious meal without sacrificing the wonderful taste. But what was every housewife's favorite kitchen appliance in the 1950s has surely evolved into a powerful and much more convenient tool that every kitchen should be equipped with.

Electric pressure cookers may have been around since 1991, but it wasn't until recently that they really reached their peak. There are a couple of electric pressure cookers currently on the market – all with smart programming and the most satisfying options – however, there is one pressure cooker in particular that stands out and casts a shadow on its competitors. The best electric pressure cooker that you can currently buy is, beyond doubt, the Power Pressure Cooker XL.

Whether you already own one and are looking for some yummy recipes for your Power Pressure Cooker, or you need a little nudge that will convince you to buy one, one thing is for sure: buying this book was definitely the smartest move.

Inside this book you will not only find over a hundred decadent and absolutely irresistible recipes (all with nutritional info) to satisfy everyone, but you will also learn what makes the Power Pressure Cooker XL so powerful and why it is worth your buck.

It may cook with pressure, but the Power Pressure Cooker XL will never leave you under pressure while cooking.

POWER PRESSURE COOKER XL – THE REVOLUTIONARY COOKING APPLIANCE

If you think that there is no way for you to whip up delicious, nutritious, and super flavorful meals with a single touch of a button, then you better think again because Power Pressure Cooker XL is about to become the definition of quick, effortless, and healthy cooking.

THE BENEFITS

So, why should you buy the Power Pressure Cooker XL? Besides the fact that the power pressure cooker XL has an incredible taste and flavor infusion technology that traps all of the cooking flavors and keeps the intensity of the taste, here are some other benefits that will definitely convince you why setting some money aside for this dream-come-true appliance of every homemaker is the best home investment to make this very instant:

It Saves Energy

Pressure cookers require less time to prepare food, wich means that they use less energy to create equally delicious meals. Say goodbye to wasting your energy with your pots, pans, and burners, because once you start cooking with the Power Pressure Cooker XL you will drastically cut back on energy. That will not only keep more money in your pocket each month, but it will also keep your stove clean at all times – since you will rarely use it.

It is Super Time Efficient

The Power Pressure Cooker XL traps the heated steam that occurs inside the pot during the process of cooking and creates a high-pressure environment that contributes to quick cooking. But besides the fact that the steam and pressure will cook your meals 70 % faster than your stove, the efficiency of the Power Pressure Cooker XL is also in the preparation method. Because it requires no other pans, skillets, or woks, and uses a single-pot cooking method, the Power Pressure Cooker XL requires no special preparations, cooks without too much hassle, and will help you serve delicious meals in a snap.

It is Economical

Not only will the Power Pressure Cooker XL save you time and money from energy, it will also allow you to cook inexpensive food to such a juicy and delightful perfection as if you used the most expensive cuts of meat and not those chops that were on sale.

It Preserves the Nutrients

Unlike the meals cooked with most of the traditional cookware, the Power Pressure Cooker XL leaves the nutrients intact. Due to the steam and pressure flow that is going on inside the Power Pressure Cooker XL during the cooking process, the food preserves its moisture and juiciness even after being cooked. The high-pressure environment locks inside all of the precious vitamins and nutrients, which adds healthier and more nutritious meals to your dinner table.

It Does Not Expose You to Harmful Substances

It is not uncommon for most cooking methods to deprive the foods of their wholesomeness and destroy the vitamins, minerals and other nutrients during the process of cooking, but they also create certain harmful compounds such as elements that can cause cancer or elevate the blood pressure. This is yet another reason why you should choose to cook your meals with the Power Pressure Cooker XL. Cooking under such pressure, the food is not only able to preserve its nutrients, but it is also not being exposed to harmful compounds.

It Has a Canning Option

Unlike the Instant Pot or other pressure cookers, this amazing extra-large kitchen appliance comes with the option for canning and preserving food. If you love using those extra fruits and veggies for creating some yummy canned good, then this is definitely the way to do it.

THE BUTTONS

If you are a proud owner of a new and shiny Power Pressure Cooker XL, you may be a little bit intimidated by the number of buttons found on the front of the cooker. Do not let its multi-functionality overwhelm you. The buttons aren't there to be overwhelming, but to actually make the cooking experience a lot more convenient for you. Once you start cooking and really 'feel' how every button works, I promise you, you won't even think about turning on your stove.

Here are the Power Pressure Cooker XL buttons and how to use them:

Delay Timer – This magical little option actually allows you to delay the cooking process. That means that you can set your pressure cooker for later in the day. For instance, if you want to have a warm dinner waiting for you when you get home from work, all you have to do is simply whip up the meal, place it inside the Power Pressure Cooker XL, and enter when you want it to start cooking. That way you can have a warm pot roast right after work, without wasting 45 minutes to cooking it Amazing, right?

Canning/Preserving – If you love canned goods, you will absolutely love this option. Canning at 12 psi (the highest pressure allowed), you can not only preserve food with this option, but you can also use it for cooking, if your recipe requires a cooking time longer than 10 minutes, that is.

Soup/Stew – This option for making soups and stews has a recommended setting for cooking time of 10 minutes. That means that if you press this button, it will pressure cook your food for 10 minutes only. However, this button also allows you to use the cook time selector and adjust the cooking time anywhere from 30 to 60 minutes.

Slow Cook – Although this is a pressure cooker, the Power Pressure Cooker XL can also replace a slow cooker as well. If you want to slow cook a meal, all you have to do is choose the "slow cook" option. The manual setting here is 2 hours, but you can adjust it to 6 or 12 hours if you need to.

Rice/Risotto – The Power Pressure Cooker XL recommends that, if you are cooking rice, you do it with this option. It has a manual setting for cooking for 6 minutes, however, you can adjust the cooking time anywhere from 18 to 25 minutes. In fact, you will find that the manual recommends cooking white rice for 6 minutes, brown rice for 18 minutes, and wild rice for 25 minutes.

Beans/Lentils – If you are making chili, or cooking beans, lentils, or similar meals, you can easily do it with this option, since its manual setting is al Ready adjusted for 5 minutes cook time. However, since you may need more time to cook your beans, depending on the type you are using, you can adjust the cooking time from 15 to 30 minutes.

Fish/Vegetable/Steam – This button has the shortest manual setting for 2 minutes cook time. You can adjust it with the cook time selector from 4 to 10 minutes.

Chicken/Meat – The manual setting is 15 minutes cook time. However, you can easily adjust it to cook your meat to perfection. Since the Power Pressure Cooker XL does not have a 'manual' button such as the Instant Pot, I find this one to be a pretty good manual replacement. With a great manual setting, this button will not only allow you to cook meat, but any kind of food you want. As you will see later in the recipes, I use this button quite a lot.

Time Adjustment – If the manual setting of the buttons doesn't offer you the right cooking option for the meal you are preparing, you can adjust it with this button. Although there are many pre-adjusted options available to choose from, this button will allow you to manually choose the cooking pressure and time.

Keep Warm/Cancel – If you want to cancel a certain function or to turn off the PPCXL, you just need to press this button. After the cooking time ends, the Power Pressure Cooker XL will automatically switch to the Keep Warm option in order to keep your meals fresh and warm until Ready to serve.

COOKING TIPS

The Power Pressure Cooker XL is not your regular kitchen appliance. It is in fact so versatile and multi-functional, and is basically a combination of many other appliances:

- It is a pressure cooker
- It is a slow cooker
- It is a sautéing pan and a stove top
- It is a rice cooker
- It is a steamer
- It is a warming pot

If you have all of these appliances crowding your kitchen, replacing some of them with the Power Pressure Cooker XL is definitely the best choice.

However, it is its very versatility that intimidates people. If you are one of the many that simply cannot figure out how to get the most out of this device, then you might want to pay attention to these net revolutionary tips:

- You can cook frozen food without defrosting. All you have to do, is simply add a couple of minutes to your cooking time.

- Do not force open the lid. You must allow for the pressure to be fully released before opening the lid. If the lid won't open, don't worry, it isn't stuck. That is just an indication that the Power Pressure Cooker XL is still pressurized and it still isn't safe to open the lid. Allow a few more minutes and try again.

- The Power Pressure Cooker XL is extremely safe to use, but only if you use it right. The best way to ensure that you will stay safe during releasing pressure and opening the lid is by ensuring that the venting knob is turned to the venting position, and by tilting the lid away from you when opening.

- The Power Pressure Cooker XL does not have a sautéing or browning function. With this appliance you can easily sauté food by choosing any of the given cooking options and cooking with the lid open. This makes the Power Pressure Cooker XL even more functional.

- Make sure not to overfill the Power Pressure Cooker XL. This will only increase the pressure and may even clog the valve. For best results, fill your Power Pressure Cooker XL up until it is 2/3 full. However, if you are cooking food that may raise or expand during the cooking process, fill it only halfway.

- Do not use too much liquid. Always follow the recipes until you have some experience under your belt and can create delicious recipes on your own. If you add more liquid than necessary, this will not only give your meals that 'rinsed' taste and dilute them, but it will also increase the time that is needed for the Power Pressure Cooker XL to go to pressure.

THE PRESSURE RELEASE

Luckily for every new user, the pressure valve of the Power Pressure Cooker XL has some pretty visible and easy-to-figure-out signs. If you line up the circle symbol, you will lock the pressure in, and if you line up the symbol of the steam coming out, you are about to release the pressure.

Now, as to when you should use the quick release or natural pressure release method, here is what you should know.

Quick – The quick pressure release method means allowing the steam to come out quickly. There really isn't a rule, and you can basically use this method anytime, however, you do have to keep in mind that if the Power Pressure Cooker XL is filled with liquid and you release the steam out quickly, spillage will most likely occur.

This method is best to use after cooking meat, seafood, or veggies.

Natural – The natural pressure release method means just the opposite – allowing the steam to come out slowly. This method is best after cooking content that is starch-high, foamy food, or food with a large liquid volume.

THE COOKING TIME

It would be remiss not to mention this, I know, but since there is a pretty detailed information about the cooking time found in your Power Pressure Cooker XL manual, I will briefly explain the basis.

Here is how long you should cook food in your Power Pressure Cooker XL:

Fresh Fish – Ready after only 2 minutes of cooking

Vegetables – Ready after only 2 minutes of cooking

Chili – usual cooking time is 30 minutes

Beef Roast – usual cooking time is 35 – 40 minutes

Pork Roast – usual cooking time is 40 – 45 minutes

Whole Chicken – usual cooking time is 20 minutes

Juicy Ribs – usual cooking time is 20 minutes

BREAKFAST RECIPES

Cheesy Eggs and Arugula in Hollandaise Sauce

Serves: 4 \ Ready in: 12 minutes

Nutritional Info:

Calories 231, Carbohydrates 8.9 g, Fiber 0.1 g, Fat 14.6 g, Protein 15.4 g

Ingredients:

4 Bread Slices, chopped

4 Eggs, whisked

½ cup Arugula, chopped

4 slices of Mozzarella Cheese

1 cup Water

1 ½ Ounces Hollandaise Sauce

Directions:

1. Place the steamer basket in your pressure cooker and pour the water inside.
2. Place the bread pieces in 4 ramekins.
3. Combine the eggs and arugula and divide this mixture between the ramekins.
4. Cover them with aluminum foil and close the lid of your pressure cooker.
5. Cook for 5 minutes on HIGH.
6. Do a quick pressure release.
7. Discard the foil and top with a slice of mozzarella and some hollandaise sauce.

Cheese and Thyme Cremini Oats

Serves: 4 \ Ready in: 20 minutes

Nutritional Info:

Calories 266, Carbohydrates 31 g, Fiber 5 g, Fat 12 g, Protein 9 g

Ingredients:

8 ounces Cremini Mushrooms, sliced

14 ounces Chicken Broth

½ Onion, diced 2 tbsp Butter

1 cup Steel-Cut Oats

½ cup grated Gouda or Cheddar Cheese

3 sprigs Thyme

½ cup Water

2 Garlic Cloves, minced

Salt and Pepper to taste

Directions:

1. Add the butter in your pressure cooker, and press CHICKEN/MEAT.
2. Add onion and mushrooms and sauté for 3 minutes.
3. Add the garlic and sauté for 1 minute.
4. Stir in the oats and cook for an additional minute.
5. Pour in the water, broth, and add thyme sprigs.
6. Season with some salt and pepper.
7. Close the lid and cook for 12 minutes.
8. Press "cancel" and release the pressure naturally.

Crustless Three-Meat Quiche

Serves: 4 \ Ready in: 30 minutes

Nutritional Info:

Calories 665.7, Carbohydrates 6.3 g, Fiber 0.3 g, Fat 39.9 g, Protein 41.8 g

Ingredients:

6 Eggs, beaten

1 cup cooked Ground Sausage

4 Bacon slices, cooked and crumbled

2 Green Onions, chopped

½ cup Milk

4 Ham Slices, diced

1½ cups Water

1 cup grated Cheddar

¼ tsp Salt, Pinch of Black Pepper

Directions:

1. Place a trivet in the pressure cooker. Pour the water in.
2. Make a sling with foil so you can remove the dish.
3. In a bowl, combine the eggs, milk, salt, and pepper.
4. Combine the sausage, cheese, bacon, ham, and onions in a baking dish.
5. Pour the egg mixture over
6. Place the dish inside the pressure cooker, cover with aluminum foil, and close the lid.
7. Cook on HIGH for about 20 minutes.
8. Turn the pressure cooker off and wait for about 10 minutes before releasing the pressure quickly.

Breakfast Vanilla Quinoa Bowl

Serves: 4 \ Ready in: 15 minutes

Nutritional Info:

Calories 186, Carbohydrates 35.7 g, Fiber 3 g, Fat 2.5 g, Protein 6 g

Ingredients:

1 cup Quinoa

2 tbsp Maple Syrup

1 tsp Vanilla Extract

1 ½ cups Water A pinch of Sea Salt

Directions:

1. Place all of the ingredients in your pressure cooker.
2. Stir to combine well.
3. Close the lid and cook for one minute on HIGH.
4. Wait for 10 minutes to do a quick pressure release.
5. Fluff with a fork.

Crispy Bacon and Egg Sandwich

Serves: 1 \ Ready in: 22 minutes

Nutritional Info:

Calories 368, Carbohydrates 31 g, Fiber 6 g, Fat 13 g, Protein 20 g

Ingredients:

2 slices of Bread

1 Egg

2 slices of Bacon

1 tsp Olive Oil

1 tbsp grated Cheese

1 cup Water

Directions:

1. Turn the pressure cooker on and choose the CHICKEN/MEAT option.
2. Add the bacon and cook until crispy.
3. Take a paper towel and wipe out the excess grease.
4. Add the water and oil.
5. Crumble the bacon in a ramekin, and crack the egg on top.
6. Sprinkle the egg with cheese.
7. Cover the ramekin with aluminum foil and place it on top of the trivet inside the pressure cooker.
8. Close the lid and cook for 6 minutes on CHICKEN/MEAT.
9. Wait to release the pressure naturally.
10. Assemble the sandwich and enjoy.

Zesty and Citrusy French Toast

Serves: 4 \ Ready in: 30 minutes

Nutritional Info:

Calories 455, Carbohydrates 64.4 g, Fiber 5.4 g, Fat 16.2 g, Protein 14.6 g

Ingredients:

Zest of 1 Orange

1 cup Water

¼ cup Granulated Sugar

2 Large Eggs

3 tbsp Butter, melted

1 ¼ cups Milk

½ tsp Vanilla Extract

⅔ loaf of Challah Bread, cut into pieces Pinch of Sea Salt

Directions:

1. Whisk together all of the ingredients -except the water and bread, in a large bowl.

2. Place the bread in the bowl and coat it with the mixture well.

3. Arrange the coated bread pieces in a baking dish.

4. Place the trivet in your pressure cooker. Pour the water inside.

5. Place the baking dish inside the pressure cooker.

6. Close the lid and cook for 25 minutes on HIGH.

7. Do a quick pressure release.

Cheddar, Ham, and Eggs Hash Bake

Serves: 4 \ Ready in: 10 minutes

Nutritional Info:

Calories 459, Carbohydrates 42.2 g, Fiber 6.1 g, Fat 20.3 g, Protein 26.8 g

Ingredients:

6 small Potatoes, shredded

6 Large Eggs, beaten

¼ cup Water

1 cup Cheddar Cheese, shredded

1 cup Ham, diced

Directions:

1. Spray some cooking spray in your pressure cooker and turn it on just to preheat it.

2. Place the shredded potatoes inside and cook until slightly browned.

3. Stir in the water.

4. In a bowl, mix the ham, cheese, and eggs, and add this mixture to the pressure cooker.

5. Stir to combine well.

6. Close the lid and cook for 1 minute on HIGH.

7. Immediately release the pressure.

Giant Coconut Pancake

Serves: 4 \ Ready in: 30 minutes

Nutritional Info:

Calories 358, Carbohydrates 39 g, Fiber 18 g, Fat 15.3 g, Protein 16.1 g

Ingredients:

1 cup Coconut Flour

1 tsp Coconut Extract

2 tbsp Honey 2 Eggs

1 ½ cups Coconut Milk

1 cup ground Almonds

½ tsp Baking Soda

Directions:

1. Whisk together the eggs and milk in a bowl.

2. Add the other ingredients gradually, while constantly whisking.

3. Spray your pressure cooker with cooking spray.

4. Pour the batter into the pressure cooker.

5. Close the lid and cook on low for 30 minutes.

6. Open the lid and transfer the pancake to a plate.

Sweet Potato, Tomato, and Onion Frittata

Serves: 4 \ Ready in: 20 minutes

Nutritional Info:

Calories 189, Carbohydrates 11.8 g, Fiber 2.6 g, Fat 11.3 g, Protein 10.9 g

Ingredients:

6 Large Eggs, beaten

1 Tomato, chopped

¼ cup Almond Milk

1 tbsp Tomato Paste

1 tbsp Olive Oil

2 tbsp Coconut Flour

1 ½ cups Water

5 tbsp chopped Onion

1 tsp minced Garlic Clove

4 ounces shredded Sweet Potatoes

Directions:

1. Whisk the wet ingredients together in a bowl (except the water).
2. Fold in the dry ingredients and stir to combine well.
3. Place the mixture in a baking dish.
4. Place a trivet in the pressure cooker and pour the water inside.
5. Place the baking dish in your pressure cooker and close the lid.
6. Cook for 18 minutes on HIGH pressure.
7. Let the pressure release naturally.

Cherry and Chocolate Oatmeal

Serves: 4 \ Ready in: 15 minutes

Nutritional Info:

Calories 283, Carbohydrates 54 g, Fiber 5.6 g, Fat 6 g, Protein 5 g

Ingredients:

3 ½ cups Water

⅛ cup Cane Sugar

1 cup Steel-Cut Oats

3 tbsp Dark Chocolate Chips

1 cup Frozen Cherries, pitted

A Pinch of Sea Salt

Directions:

1. Place all of the ingredients except the chocolate in your pressure cooker.
2. Stir well to combine. Close the lid.
3. Choose the CHICKEN/MEAT option (trust me on this) and cook for 12 minutes.
4. Release the pressure quickly. Stir in the chocolate chips.

Chorizo and Kale Egg Casserole

Serves: 4 \ Ready in: 30 minutes

Nutritional Info:

Calories 426, Carbohydrates 13.2 g, Fiber 1.6 g, Fat 30.2 g, Protein 24.3 g

Ingredients:

8 ounces Chorizo, cooked

1 tbsp Coconut Oil

6 Eggs

¾ cup sliced Leek

1 ½ cups Water

1 cup Kale, chopped

1 Sweet Potato, shredded

1 tsp minced Garlic

Directions:

1. Turn on your Pressure Cooker and melt the coconut oil.
2. Add garlic, kale, and leeks, and sauté them for a couple of minutes, until soft.
3. Meanwhile grease a baking dish.
4. Place the veggies in the baking dish.
5. Beat the eggs and pour them over the veggies. Stir in chorizo and potato.
6. Place the trivet in the pressure cooker and pour the water inside.
7. Place the baking dish inside the pressure cooker, close the lid, and cook on CHICKEN/MEAT for 25 minutes.
8. Do a quick pressure release.

Banana and Cinnamon French Toast

Serves: 6 \ Ready in: 30 minutes

Nutritional Info:

Calories 313, Carbohydrates 39 g, Fiber 2 g, Fat 15 g, Protein 8 g

Ingredients:

1 ½ tsp Cinnamon

¼ tsp Vanilla Extract

6 Bread Slices, cubed

4 Bananas, sliced

2 tbsp Brown Sugar

1 tbsp White Sugar

½ cup Milk

¼ cup Pecans, chopped

3 Eggs

¼ cup Cream Cheese, softened

2 tbsp cold and sliced Butter

¾ cup Water

Directions:

1. Grease a 1 ½ - quart baking dish and arrange half of the bread cubes.
2. Top the bread with half of the banana slices.
3. Sprinkle half of the brown sugar over.
4. Spread the cream cheese over the bananas.
5. Arrange the rest of the bread cubes and banana slices over.
6. Sprinkle with brown sugar and top with pecans.
7. Top with the butter slices.
8. Whisk together the eggs, white sugar, milk, cinnamon, and vanilla in a bowl.
9. Pour the mixture over.
10. Place the trivet inside the pressure cooker and add the water.
11. Place the baking dish inside the pressure cooker, close the lid, and cook on CHICKEN/MEAT for 25 minutes.
12. Release the pressure quickly.

SOUPS AND STEWS

Ham and Pea Soup

Serves: 6 \ Ready in: 30 minutes

Nutritional Info:

Calories 276.6, Carbohydrates 49.9 g, Fiber 20.5 g, Fat 1 g, Protein 19.1 g

Ingredients:

1 Onion, diced

1 pound Split Peas, dried

2 Carrots, diced

8 cups Water

2 Celery Stalks, diced

1 pound Ham Chunks

1 ½ tsp dried Thyme

Directions:

1. Combine all of the ingredients in your Pressure Cooker.
2. The pot shouldn't be more than half full.
3. Close the lid and cook 20 minutes on HIGH pressure.
4. If you don't like the density, cook for additional 10 minutes.

Tortellini Minestrone Soup

Serves: 6 \ Ready in: 15 minutes

Nutritional Info:

Calories 245, Carbohydrates 34.2 g, Fiber 4.3 g, Fat 9.1 g, Protein 7.4 g

Ingredients:

1 Onion, diced

2 Carrots, diced

1 tbsp minced Garlic

2 tbsp Olive Oil

4 cups Veggie Broth

24 ounces jarred Spaghetti Sauce

1 tsp Sugar

2 Celery Stalks, sliced

¼ tsp Black Pepper

1½ tsp Italian Seasoning

14 ounces canned diced Tomatoes

8 ounces dry Cheese Tortellini

Directions:

1. Add the olive oil to your pressure cooker and turn it on to heat it.
2. Add the onions, garlic, celery, and carrots, and cook until they start to 'sweat'.
3. Stir in the rest of the ingredients.
4. Close the lid and cook for 5 minutes on HIGH pressure.
5. Do a quick pressure release.
6. Check the tortellini. If they are too 'al dente' for your liking, you can continue boiling them with the lid off for a few more minutes.

Mushroom and Beef Stew

Serves: 4 \ Ready in: 20 minutes

Nutritional Info:

Calories 527, Carbohydrates 50 g, Fiber 6.3 g, Fat 17.7 g, Protein 44.6 g

Ingredients:

2 tbsp Canola Oil

1 tsp dried Parsley

1 Onion, chopped

1 ½ pound Beef, cut into pieces

4 Red Potatoes, cut into chunks

4 Carrots, cut into chunks

8 Button Mushrooms, sliced

10 ounces Golden Mushroom Soup

12 ounces Water

Directions:

1. Heat the oil in the pressure cooker.
2. Add meat and brown it on all sides.
3. Stir in the remaining ingredients.
4. Close the lid and cook for 15 minutes on high pressure.
5. Release the pressure naturally.

Chicken Enchilada Soup

Serves: 8 \ Ready in: 30 minutes

Nutritional Info:

Calories 397, Carbohydrates 46 g, Fiber 3 g, Fat 5 g, Protein 45 g

Ingredients:

8 cups cubed Butternut Squash

1 pound boneless and skinless Chicken Breasts

8 ounces canned Tomato Soup

2 tsp Cumin

1 Onion, chopped

3 ½ ounces canned chopped Chillies

2 tsp Taco Seasoning

2 tsp Salt

3 Russet Potatoes, quartered

3 Garlic Cloves, minced

4 cups Chicken Broth

30 ounces canned Cannellini Beans

1 Red Bell Pepper, chopped

Directions:

1. Place all of the ingredients in your pressure cooker.
2. Stir to combine well.
3. Close the lid and cook for 20 minutes on CHICKEN/MEAT.
4. Release the pressure naturally.
5. Remove the chicken from the cooker.
6. With a hand blender, blend the soup until smooth.
7. Shred the chicken with two forks and return the meat to the soup.

Lentil Soup

Serves: 4 \ Ready in: 25 minutes

Nutritional Info:

Calories 259, Carbohydrates 35.4 g, Fiber 16.3 g, Fat 7.5 g, Protein 13.3 g

Ingredients:

4 Garlic Cloves, minced

1 tsp Cumin

4 cups Veggie Broth

½ Onion, chopped

2 Celery Stalks, chopped

2 Carrots, chopped

1 cup dry Lentils

2 Bay Leaves

2 tbsp Olive Oil

Salt and Pepper, to taste

Directions:

1. Heat the olive oil in your pressure cooker.
2. Add onions, garlic, and carrots, and cook until they start to 'sweat'.
3. Add celery and sauté for one more minute.
4. Stir in the remaining ingredients.
5. Close the lid and cook for 20 minutes on HIGH.
6. Release the pressure naturally.

Irish Lamb Stew

Serves: 4 \ Ready in: 25 minutes

Nutritional Info:

Calories 321, Carbohydrates 28.8 g, Fiber 3.9 g, Fat 11.4 g, Protein 24.8 g

Ingredients:

1 pound Lamb, cut into pieces

1 Onion, sliced

2 tbsp Cornstarch or Arrowroot

1 ½ tbsp Olive Oil

2 Sweet Potatoes, cut into cubes

3 Carrots, chopped

2 ½ cups Veggie Broth

½ tsp dried Thyme

Directions:

1. Heat the olive oil in your pressure cooker.
2. Cook the lamb until browned on all sides.
3. Add all of the remaining ingredients, except the cornstarch, and stir well to combine.
4. Close the lid and cook on HIGH for 11 minutes.
5. Let the pressure release naturally for 11 more minutes.
6. Whisk the cornstarch with a little bit of water and stir it into the stew.
7. Cook on HIGH for an additional minute.
8. Do a quick pressure release.

Navy Bean and Ham Shank Soup

Serves: 12 \ Ready in: 8 hours and 30 minutes

Nutritional Info:

Calories 641.2, Carbohydrates 48.7 g, Fiber 18.7 g, Fat 34.1 g, Protein 35.9 g

Ingredients:

½ cup Vegetable Oil

4 cups dried Navy Beans

3 pounds Ham Shank

2 Onions, chopped

4 Carrots, sliced

½ cup minced Green Pepper

3 Quarts Water

2 cups Tomato Sauce

4 Celery Stalks, chopped

2 Garlic Cloves, minced

Salt and Pepper, to taste

Directions:

1. Soak the beans in the vegetable oil with some salt and pepper overnight.
2. Drain them well.
3. Place the beans in the pressure cooker and add all of the remaining ingredients.
4. Stir well to combine.
5. Close the lid and cook for about 20 minutes on HIGH pressure.
6. Release the pressure naturally.

Skim and Fast Miso and Tofu Soup

Serves: 4 \ Ready in: 12 minutes

Nutritional Info:

Calories 46, Carbohydrates 3.7 g, Fiber 1 g, Fat 1.7 g, Protein 3.8 g

Ingredients:

4 cups Water

½ cup Corn

2 tbsp Miso Paste

1 Onion, sliced

1 tsp Wakame Flakes

1 cup Silken Tofu, cubed

2 Celery Stalks, chopped

2 Carrots, chopped

Soy Sauce, to taste

Directions:

1. Combine all of the ingredients except the miso paste and soy sauce in your pressure cooker.
2. Close the lid and cook for 7 minutes on CHICKEN/MEAT.
3. Release the pressure quickly.
4. Mix the miso paste with one cup of the broth and stir it into the soup.
5. Add some soy sauce and stir.

Pomodoro Soup

Serves: 8 \ Ready in: 15 minutes

Nutritional Info:

Calories 314, Carbohydrates 16 g, Fiber 2 g, Fat 23 g, Protein 11 g

Ingredients:

3 pounds Tomatoes, peeled and quartered

1 Carrot, diced

1 Onion, diced

¼ cup Fresh Basil

1 cup Half & Half

1 tbsp Tomato Paste

3 tbsp Butter

½ tsp Salt

½ tsp Pepper

29 ounces Chicken Broth

½ cup grated Parmesan Cheese

1 tsp minced Garlic

Directions:

1. Melt the butter in your Power Pressure Cooker XL and cook the onions, celery, and carrots until they start to 'sweat'.
2. Add garlic and cook for 30 more seconds.
3. Stir in the remaining ingredients, except the cream and cheese.
4. Close the lid and cook for 6 minutes on SOUP/STEW.
5. Press "cancel" and wait for 5 minutes before doing a quick pressure release.
6. Stir in the half & half and parmesan cheese.

Pressure Cooked Chili

Serves: 4 \ Ready in: 30 minutes

Nutritional Info:

Calories 388.5, Carbohydrates 15.2 g, Fiber 2.9 g, Fat 27.6 g, Protein 22 g

Ingredients:

1 pound Ground Beef

½ cup Beef Broth

1 Onion, diced

1 tbsp Olive Oil

28 ounces canned Tomatoes

½ tbsp Cumin

1 ½ tbsp Chili Powder

1 tsp Garlic Powder

2 tbsp Tomato Paste

Directions:

1. Heat the olive oil in your Power Pressure Cooker XL.
2. Add the beef and cook until browned, about 4 minutes.
3. Add the onion and cook for 2 more minutes.
4. Add cumin, chili, garlic powder, tomato paste, and cook for an additional minute.
5. Stir in the tomatoes and beef broth.
6. Close the lid and cook for 25 minutes on BEANS/LENTILS.
7. Do a quick pressure release.

Pumpkin, Corn, and Chicken Chowder

Serves: 4 \ Ready in: 15 minutes

Nutritional Info:

Calories 314, Carbohydrates 16.6 g, Fiber 5.8 g, Fat 21.1 g, Protein 14.7 g

Ingredients:

2 Chicken Breasts

2 cups Corn, canned or frozen

1 Onion, diced

¼ tsp Pepper

½ cup Half & Half

15 ounces Pumpkin Puree

29 ounces Chicken Broth

½ tsp dried Oregano

1 Garlic Clove, minced

Pinch of Nutmeg

Pinch of Red Pepper Flakes

2 Potatoes, cubed

2 tbsp Butter

Directions:

1. Turn your Power Pressure Cooker XL on and choose the CHICKEN/MEAT setting. Melt the butter and sauté the onion until translucent.

2. Add garlic and cook for an additional minute.

3. Add pumpkin puree, the broth, and all the seasonings.

4. Stir in potatoes and chicken, close the lid and cook for 5 minutes.

5. Do a quick pressure release.

6. Add the half & half and corn.

Spicy Beef and Potato Soup

Serves: 8 \ Ready in: 25 minutes

Nutritional Info:

Calories 242.6, Carbohydrates 27.1 g, Fiber 4.2 g, Fat 9.3 g, Protein 14.7 g

Ingredients:

1 pound Ground Beef

4 cups Water

24 ounces Tomato Sauce

2 cups Fresh Corn

2 tsp Salt

4 cups cubed Potatoes

1 Onion, chopped

½ tsp Hot Pepper Sauce

1 ½ tsp Black Pepper

Directions:

1. Spray some cooking spray in your Power Pressure Cooker XL.
2. Add the beef and cook until browned.
3. Add onions and cook for 2 more minutes.
4. Stir in the remaining ingredients.
5. Close the lid and cook on HIGH for about 6 minutes.
6. Release the pressure naturally.

Creamy Curried Cauliflower Soup

Serves: 4 \ Ready in: 18 minutes

Nutritional Info:

Calories 115.6, Carbohydrates 19.5 g, Fiber 4.1 g, Fat 2.8 g, Protein 2.8 g

Ingredients:

1 Cauliflower Head, chopped

1 tbsp Curry Powder

½ tsp Turmeric Powder

1 Sweet Potato, diced

1 Onion, diced

1 Carrot, diced

1 cup Coconut Milk

2 cups Veggie Broth

½ tbsp Coconut Oil

Directions:

1. Melt the coconut oil in your Power Pressure Cooker XL.
2. Add onions and carrots and sauté for 3 minutes.
3. Add the rest of the ingredients in the pressure cooker.
4. Stir to combine well.
5. Close the lid, choose the SOUP/STEW mode, and cook for 15 minutes.
6. Release the pressure naturally.
7. Blend with a hand blender until smooth.

POULTRY RECIPES

Hot and Spicy Shredded Chicken

Serves: 4 \ Ready in: 30 minutes

Nutritional Info:

Calories 307.4, Carbohydrates 12.1 g, Fiber 1.2 g, Fat 10.2 g, Protein 38.3 g

Ingredients:

1 ½ pound boneless and skinless Chicken Breast

2 cups diced Tomatoes

½ tsp Oregano

2 Green Chilies, seeded and chopped

½ tsp Paprika

2 tbsp Coconut Sugar

½ cup Salsa

1 tsp Cumin

2 tbsp Olive Oil

Directions:

1. In a small bowl, combine the oil with all of the spices.
2. Rub the chicken breast with the spicy marinade.
3. Place the meat in your pressure cooker.
4. Add the diced tomatoes. Close the lid and cook for 20 minutes on HIGH.
5. Transfer the chicken to a cutting board and shred it.
6. Return the shredded meat tot the Power Pressure Cooker XL.
7. Choose the "slow cook" setting and cook for 10 more minutes.

Teriyaki Chicken Under Pressure

Serves: 8 \ Ready in: 20 minutes

Nutritional Info:

Calories 352, Carbohydrates 31 g, Fiber 1.2 g, Fat 11.4 g, Protein 30.7 g

Ingredients:

1 cup Chicken Broth

¾ cup Brown Sugar

2 tbsp ground Ginger

1 tsp Pepper

3 pounds Boneless and Skinless Chicken Thighs

¼ cup Apple Cider Vinegar

¾ cup low-sodium Soy Sauce

20 ounces canned Pineapple, crushed

2 tbsp Garlic Powder

Directions:

1. Place the chicken in your pressure cooker.
2. Combine all of the remaining ingredients in a bowl.
3. Pour the sauce over the meat.
4. Close the lid, choose the CHICKEN/MEAT option and cook for 20 minutes.
5. Wait 2 minutes before releasing the pressure quickly.

Creamy Turkey and Mushrooms

Serves: 4 \ Ready in: 25 minutes

Nutritional Info:

Calories 192, Carbohydrates 5 g, Fiber 1 g, Fat 12 g, Protein 15 g

Ingredients:

20 ounces Turkey Breasts, boneless and skinless

6 ounces White Button Mushrooms, sliced

3 tbsp chopped Shallots

½ tsp dried Thyme

1/3 cup dry White Wine

2/3 cup Chicken Stock

1 Garlic Clove, minced

2 tbsp Olive Oil

3 tbsp Heavy Cream

1 ½ tbsp Cornstarch

Salt and Pepper, to taste

Directions:

1. Tie the turkey breast with a kitchen string horizontally, leaving approximately 2 inches apart.
2. Season the meat with salt and pepper.
3. Heat half of the olive oil in your Power Pressure Cooker XL.
4. Add the turkey and cook for about 3 minutes on each side.
5. Transfer to a plate.
6. Heat the remaining oil and cook shallots, thyme, garlic, and mushrooms until soft.
7. Add white wine and scrape up the brown bits from the bottom.

8. When the alcohol evaporates, return the turkey to the pressure cooker.

9. Close the lid and cook for 22 minutes on CHICKEN/MEAT.

10. Combine the heavy cream and cornstarch in a small bowl.

11. Open the lid and stir in the mixture.

12. Bring the sauce to a boil, then turn the cooker off.

13. Slice the turkey in half and serve topped with the creamy mushroom sauce.

Simple Pressure Cooked Whole Chicken

Serves: 4 \ Ready in: 30 minutes

Nutritional Info:

Calories 376, Carbohydrates 0 g, Fiber 0 g, Fat 30 g, Protein 25.1 g

Ingredients:

1 2-pound Whole Chicken

2 tbsp Olive Oil

1 ½ cups Water

Salt and Pepper, to taste

Directions:

1. Rinse the chicken and pat dry.

2. Season with some salt and pepper.

3. Heat the oil in your Power Pressure Cooker XL and cook the chicken until browned on all sides.

4. Add a rack inside your pressure cooker and pour the water inside.

5. Place the chicken on the rack.

6. Close the lid and cook for 20 minutes on HIGH pressure.

7. Do a quick pressure release.

Turkey and Potatoes in Buffalo Sauce

Serves: 4 \ Ready in: 30 minutes

Nutritional Info:

Calories 377.5, Carbohydrates 32.1 g, Fiber 4.2 g, Fat 9.3 g, Protein 14.7 g

Ingredients:

3 tbsp Olive Oil, Coconut Oil or Ghee

4 tbsp Buffalo Sauce (use dairy-free)

1 pound Sweet Potatoes, cut into cubes

1 ½ pounds Turkey Breast, cut into pieces

½ tsp Garlic Powder

1 Onion, diced

Directions:

1. Heat one tbsp of olive oil in your pressure cooker.
2. Add the onions and sauté for about 3 minutes.
3. Stir in the remaining ingredients.
4. Close the lid, select the CHICKEN/MEAT setting, and cook for no longer than 15 minutes. Do a quick pressure release.

Fall-Off-Bone Drumsticks

Serves: 3 \ Ready in: 22 minutes

Nutritional Info:

Calories 454, Carbohydrates 6.7 g, Fiber 1.4 g, Fat 27.2 g, Protein 43.2 g

Ingredients:

1 tbsp Olive Oil

6 Skinless Chicken Drumsticks

4 Garlic Cloves, smashed

½ Red Bell Pepper, diced

½ Onion, diced

2 tbsp Tomato Paste

2 cups Water

Directions:

1. Heat the olive oil in you Power Pressure Cooker XL.
2. Add onion and bell pepper and cook for about 4 minutes.
3. Add garlic and cook until it becomes golden.
4. Combine the tomato paste with water and pour it into the Power Pressure Cooker XL.
5. Arrange the drumsticks inside.
6. Close the lid and cook for about 15 minutes on HIGH pressure.
7. Release the pressure naturally.

Chicken Piccata

Serves: 6 \ Ready in: 20 minutes

Nutritional Info:

Calories 318, Carbohydrates 15 g, Fiber 0.8 g, Fat 19.2 g, Protein 19.4 g

Ingredients:

6 Chicken Breast Halves

¼ cup Olive Oil

⅓ cup Freshly Squeezed Lemon Juice

1 tbsp Sherry Wine

½ cup Flour

4 Shallots, chopped

3 Garlic Cloves, crushed

¾ cup Chicken Broth

1 tsp dried Basil

2 tsp Salt

¼ cup grated Parmesan Cheese

1 tbsp Flour

¼ cup Sour Cream

1 cup Pimento Olives minced

¼ tsp White Pepper

Directions:

1. Dust chicken with flour. Heat the olive oil in your Power Pressure Cooker XL and cook the chicken until browned on all sides.
2. Remove the chicken from the cooker.
3. Sauté shallots, and garlic for a couple of minutes.
4. Add sherry, broth, lemon juice, salt, olives, basil, and pepper.
5. Return the chicken to the cooker.
6. Close the lid and cook on CHICKEN/MEAT for 10 minutes.
7. Stir in sour cream and parmesan. Close the lid and cook for an additional minute.

Salsa and Lime Chicken with Rice

Serves: 4 \ Ready in: 25 minutes

Nutritional Info:

Calories 403, Carbohydrates 44.2 g, Fiber 1.6 g, Fat 16.8 g, Protein 19 g

Ingredients:

¼ cup Lime Juice

3 tbsp Olive Oil

½ cup Salsa

2 Frozen Chicken Breasts, boneless and skinless

½ tsp Garlic Powder

1 cup Rice

1 cup Water

½ tsp Pepper

½ cup Mexican Cheese Blend

½ cup Tomato Sauce

Directions:

1. Combine the chicken, lime juice, salt, garlic powder, olive oil, tomato sauce, and pepper in your Power Pressure Cooker XL.

2. Close the lid and cook on HIGH pressure for about 13 minutes.

3. An inserted thermometer should read 165 degrees F minimum.

4. Release the pressure naturally and transfer the chicken to a plate.

5. Add the rice in the cooking liquid and add the water (the total liquid in the pressure cooker should be about 2 cups so add a little bit more water if needed).

6. Close the lid and cook for 12 minutes on HIGH.

7. Serve rice with chicken.

Creamy and Garlicky Italian Spinach Chicken

Serves: 4 \ Ready in: 15 minutes

Nutritional Info:

Calories 455, Carbohydrates 3 g, Fiber 2 g, Fat 26 g, Protein 57 g

Ingredients:

1 cup chopped Spinach

2 pounds Chicken Breasts, boneless and skinless, cut in half

½ cup Chicken Broth

2 Garlic Cloves, minced

2 tbsp Olive Oil

¾ cup Heavy Cream

½ cup Sun-Dried Tomatoes

2 tsp Italian Seasoning

½ cup Parmesan Chicken

½ tsp Salt

Directions:

1. Rub the meat with the oil, garlic, salt, and seasonings.
2. Add the chicken in your Power Pressure Cooker XL and brown it on all sides.
3. Pour the broth in, close the lid and cook for 4 minutes.
4. Release the pressure quickly and add the cream.
5. Simmer for 5 minutes with the lid off, and then stir in the cheese.
6. Stir in tomatoes and spinach and cook just until the spinach wilts.

Cherry Tomato, Olive, and Basil Chicken Casserole

Serves: 4 \ Ready in: 30 minutes

Nutritional Info:

Calories 337 Carbohydrates 11.8 g, Fiber 2.6 g, Fat 21.4 g, Protein 27 g

Ingredients:

8 small Chicken Thighs

½ cup Green Olives

1 pound Cherry Tomatoes

1 cup Water

A handful of Fresh Basil Leaves

1 ½ tsp minced Garlic

1 tsp dried Oregano

1 tbsp Olive Oil

Directions:

1. Heat the olive oil in your Power Pressure Cooker XL.
2. Cook the chicken about 2 minutes per side.
3. Place the tomatoes in a plastic bag and smash them with a meat pounder.
4. Remove the chicken from the cooker.
5. Combine tomatoes, garlic, water, and oregano in the Power Pressure Cooker XL.
6. Top with the browned chicken.
7. Close the lid and cook for 12 minutes on HIGH pressure.
8. Stir in the basil and olives.

RED MEAT RECIPES

Lamb Shanks Braised Under Pressure

Serves: 4 \ Ready in: 30 minutes

Nutritional Info:

Calories 804, Carbohydrates 19 g, Fiber 2.9 g, Fat 42.9 g, Protein 73.7 g

Ingredients:

4-6 Lamb Shanks

3 Carrots, sliced

2 Tomatoes, peeled and quartered

1 Garlic Clove, crushed

1 tbsp chopped Fresh Oregano

¼ cup plus 4 tsp Flour

8 tsp Olive Oil

1 Onion, chopped

¾ cup Red Wine

¼ cup Beef Broth

8 tsp Cold Water

Directions:

1. Place ¼ cup of the flour and the lamb shanks in a plastic bag.

2. Shake until you coat the shanks well. Discard the excess flour.

3. Heat 4 tsp of the oil in your Power Pressure Cooker XL. Brown the shanks on both sides. Set aside.

4. Heat the remaining olive oil and sauté the onions, garlic and carrots for a couple of minutes. Stir in tomatoes, wine, broth, and oregano.

5. Return the shanks to the cooker.

6. Close the lid and cook for 25 minutes on HIGH pressure. Release the pressure quickly. Whisk together the remaining flour and water.

7. Stir this mixture into the lamb sauce and cook with the lid off until it thickens.

Sticky Baby Back Ribs

Serves: 4 \ Ready in: 30 minutes

Nutritional Info:

Calories 228.3, Carbohydrates 36.6 g, Fiber 0.7 g, Fat 7 g, Protein 8 g

Ingredients:

3 pounds Baby Beef Racks

2 tsp Olive Oil

1 cup Beer

½ tsp Salt

12 ounces Barbecue Sauce

½ tsp Onion Powder

¼ tsp Paprika

¼ tsp Garlic Powder

¼ tsp Black Pepper

Directions:

1. Cut the ribs into pieces. Mix together all of the spices in a small bowl. Rub the spice mixture over the meat.

2. Heat the oil in your pressure cooker and brown the meat on all sides.

3. Insert the rack, arrange the ribs on top, and pour the beer over.

4. Close the lid and cook for 25 minutes on HIGH heat. Let the pressure release naturally.

5. Brush the barbecue sauce over the ribs. Simmer with the lid off for a couple of minutes until sticky.

Saucy Beef Tips and Rice

Serves: 4 \ Ready in: 25 minutes

Nutritional Info:

Calories 358.5, Carbohydrates 64.1 g, Fiber 1.9 g, Fat 7.4 g, Protein 7.7 g

Ingredients:

2 tsp Salt

2 pounds Sirloin Steaks, cut into pieces

2 tbsp Vegetable Oil

2 Onions, chopped

½ tsp Paprika

¼ tsp Mustard Powder

½ tsp Black Pepper

3 tbsp Flour

2 Garlic Cloves, minced

4 cups cooked Rice

10 ½ ounces Beef Consommé

Directions:

1. In a Ziploc bag, place flour, mustard powder, salt, pepper, and paprika.
2. Add the beef cubes and shake the bag to coat them well.
3. Heat the oil in you Power Pressure Cooker XL and brown the meat on all sides.
4. Add the onions and garlic and cook until translucent.
5. Stir in the beef consommé.
6. Close the lid and cook for 20 minutes over HIGH pressure.
7. Release the pressure naturally and simmer with the lid off until you reach your preferred consistency.

Worcestershire Pork Chops

Serves: 6 \ Ready in: 20 minutes

Nutritional Info:

Calories 785.2, Carbohydrates 25.9 g, Fiber 3.3 g, Fat 41.5 g, Protein 73.4 g

Ingredients:

1 Onion, diced

8 Pork Chops

¼ cup Butter

3 tbsp Worcestershire Sauce

1 cup Water

4 Potatoes, diced

Salt and Pepper, to taste

Directions:

1. Melt half of the butter in your pressure cooker.
2. Brown the pork chops on all sides and season with salt and pepper. Set aside.
3. Add the rest of the butter in the Power Pressure Cooker XL.
4. Add onions and sauté for 2 or 3 minutes.
5. Add potatoes and stir in the water and Worcestershire sauce.
6. Add the pork chops to the cooker again.
7. Close the lid and cook on HIGH pressure for 15 minutes.
8. Release the pressure naturally.

Potted Rump Steak

Serves: 15 \ Ready in: 30 minutes

Nutritional Info:

Calories 615.8, Carbohydrates 11.1 g, Fiber 2.4 g, Fat 34.3 g, Protein 59 g

Ingredients:

3 tbsp Olive Oil

3 Bay Leaves

9 pounds Rump Steak

2 cups diced Celery

1 tsp Salt

3 Onions, chopped

2 cups sliced Mushrooms

18 ounces canned Tomato Paste

10 ½ ounces Beef Broth

1 ½ cups Dry Red Wine

Directions:

1. Heat the oil in your Power Pressure Cooker XL and brown the steak on all sides.
2. Add the vegetables and stir in all of the seasonings.
3. Combine the paste with the wine and broth.
4. Add this mixture to the cooker.
5. Close the lid and cook for about 25 minutes on HIGH pressure.
6. Check the meat and cook for a little bit more if you don't like the density or you want your meat overcooked.

Sloppy Joes and Coleslaw

Serves: 6 \ Ready in: 20 minutes

Nutritional Info:

Calories 180, Carbohydrates 18 g, Fiber 3.5 g, Fat g, Protein 3.5 g

Ingredients:

1 cup chopped Tomatoes

1 Onion, chopped

1 Carrot, chopped

1 pound Ground Beef

1 Bell Pepper, chopped

½ cup Rolled Oats

4 tbsp Apple Cider Vinegar

1 tbsp Olive Oil

4 tbsp Tomato Paste

1 cup Water

2 tsp Garlic Powder

1 tbsp Worcestershire Sauce

1 ½ tsp Salt

Coleslaw:

½ chopped Red Onion

1 tbsp Honey

½ head Cabbage, sliced

2 Carrots, grated

2 tbsp Apple Cider Vinegar

1 tbsp Dijon Mustard

Directions:

1. Heat the olive oil in your pressure cooker and brown the meat.
2. Add onions, carrots, pepper, garlic powder, and salt, and sauté until soft. Stir in tomatoes, vinegar, Worcestershire sauce, water, and tomato paste.
3. When starting to boil, stir in the oats.
4. Close the lid and cook for about 12 minutes on HIGH pressure.
5. Release the pressure quickly and simmer with the lid off until thickened to your liking.
6. Mix all of the slaw ingredeients in a large bowl. Serve the sloppy joes with the slaw.

Pot Roast in Peach Sauce

Serves: 8 \ Ready in: 30 minutes

Nutritional Info:

Calories 324.3, Carbohydrates 21.6 g, Fiber 1 g, Fat 10.4 g, Protein 37.4 g

Ingredients:

3-4 pounds Beef Roast

1 Onion, peeled and quartered

3 ½ tbsp Cornstarch

1 ½ quarts Peach Juice

3 ounces Cold Water

2 Garlic Cloves, minced

2 tbsp Olive Oil

Salt and Pepper, to taste

Directions:

1. Heat the olive oil in your Power Pressure Cooker XL. Add the pot roast and brown on all sides.

2. Add the onions and garlic and cook for a minute or two.

3. Cover the pot roast with the peach juice (add a little bit more juice if needed).

4. Close the lid and cook for 30 minutes on HIGH pressure.

5. Release the pressure naturally. Transfer the roast to a plate and leave to rest.

6. Whisk the water and cornstarch together and stir into the juice in the cooker.

7. Simmer with the lid off until the gravy thickens.

8. Slice the meat and pour the gravy over.

Shredded Beef the Caribbean Way

Serves: 4 \ Ready in: 30 minutes

Nutritional Info:

Calories 739.2, Carbohydrates 1.3 g, Fiber 0.2 g, Fat 56.7 g, Protein 56.9 g

Ingredients:

2 pounds Beef Roast

½ tsp Turmeric

1 tsp grated Ginger

¼ cup Water

4 Whole Cloves

1 tsp dried Thyme

1 tsp Garlic Powder

Directions:

1. Combine the turmeric, garlic, thyme, and ginger in a small bowl.

2. Rub the mixture into the beef. Stick the cloves into the beef roast.

3. Place the beer inside your Power Pressure Cooker XL and pour the water around it.

4. Cook for about 30 minutes on HIGH pressure. Shred the meat.

Smokey Pork Roast

Serves: 4 \ Ready in: 30 minutes

Nutritional Info:

Calories 767, Carbohydrates 2.2 g, Fiber 0.5 g, Fat 41.9 g, Protein 89 g

Ingredients:

2 pounds Pork Meat

1 tsp Oregano

1 tsp Cumin

1 tsp Liquid Smoke

1 tsp Coconut Sugar

1 tbsp Coconut Oil

1 tsp ground Ginger

½ cup Beef Broth

1 tsp Paprika

½ tsp Pepper

Directions:

1. Place all of the spices in a small bowl and stir to combine.
2. Rub the meat with the spice mixture.
3. Melt the coconut oil in your Power Pressure Cooker XL.
4. Add the pork and cook until browned on all sides.
5. Combine the liquid smoke and broth and pour over the pork.
6. Close the lid and cook for about 30 minutes on HIGH pressure.
7. Let the pressure release naturally.

Beef with Cabbage, Potatoes, and Carrots

Serves: 6 \ Ready in: 30 minutes

Nutritional Info:

Calories 712, Carbohydrates 55 g, Fiber 10.7 g, Fat 36.4 g, Protein 41.6 g

Ingredients:

6 Potatoes, peeled and quartered

4 Carrots, cut into pieces

2 ½ pounds Beef Brisket

1 Cabbage Head

3 Garlic Cloves, quartered

3 Turnips, chopped

2 Bay Leaves

4 cups of Water

Directions:

1. Pour the water into your Power Pressure Cooker XL.
2. Add the garlic and bay leaves.
3. Close the lid and cook for 24 minutes on HIGH pressure.
4. Release the pressure quickly.
5. Add the veggies.
6. Close the lid and cook for 6 more minutes

Beef and Cheese Taco Pie

Serves: 4 \ Ready in: 20 minutes

Nutritional Info:

Calories 363, Carbohydrates 29 g, Fiber 6 g, Fat 19 g, Protein 25 g

Ingredients:

1 package Corn Tortillas

1 packet of Taco Seasoning

1 pound Ground Beef

12 ounces Mexican Cheese Blend

¼ cup Refried Beans

1 cup Water

Directions:

1. Pour the water in your Power Pressure Cooker XL.
2. Combine the meat with the seasoning.
3. Place one tortilla in the bottom of a pan and place it in your cooker.
4. Top with beans, beef, and cheese.
5. Top with another tortilla.
6. Repeat the process until you use up all of the ingredients.
7. The final layer should be a tortilla.
8. Close the lid. Cook for 12 minutes on CHICKEN/MEAT.
9. Remove the pan from the Power Pressure Cooker XL.

Herbed Lamb Roast with Potatoes

Serves: 4 \ Ready in: 30 minutes

Nutritional Info:

Calories 739.2, Carbohydrates 1.3 g, Fiber 0.2 g, Fat 56.7 g, Protein 56.9 g

Ingredients:

6 pounds Leg of Lamb

1 tsp dried Sage

1 tsp dried Marjoram

1 Bay Leaf, crushed

1 tsp dried Thyme

3 Garlic Cloves, minced

3 pounds Potatoes, cut into pieces

2 tbsp Olive Oil

3 tbsp Arrowroot Powder

⅓ cup Water

2 cups Chicken Broth

Salt and Pepper, to taste

Directions:

1. Heat the oil in your Power Pressure Cooker XL.
2. Combine the herbs with some salt and pepper and rub the mixture into the meat.
3. Brown the lamb on all sides. Pour the broth around the meat, close the lid, and cook for 60 minutes on CHICKEN/MEAT.
4. Release the pressure quickly and add the potatoes.
5. Close the lid and cook for 12 more minutes. Transfer the meat and potatoes to a plate. Combine the water and arrowroot and stir the mixture into the pot sauce.
6. Pour the gravy over the meat and potatoes and enjoy.

SEAFOOD RECIPES

Clams in White Wine

Serves: 4 \ Ready in: 17 minutes

Nutritional Info:

Calories 224.4, Carbohydrates 5.8 g, Fiber 0.1 g, Fat 14.6 g, Protein 15.6 g

Ingredients:

¼ cup White Wine

2 cups Veggie Broth

¼ cup chopped Basil

¼ cup Olive Oil

2 ½ pounds Clams

2 tbsp Lemon Juice

2 Garlic Cloves, minced

Directions:

1. Heat the olive oil in your Power Pressure Cooker XL.
2. Add garlic and cook for one minute.
3. Add wine, basil, lemon juice, and veggie broth.
4. Bring the mixture to a boil and boil for one minute.
5. Add your steaming basket, and place the clams inside.
6. Close the lid and cook for 4 minutes on HIGH pressure.
7. Place the clams on a plate and drizzle with the cooking liquid.

Almond-Crusted Tilapia

Serves: 4 \ Ready in: 10 minutes

Nutritional Info:

Calories 326.8, Carbohydrates 4.1 g, Fiber 2.8 g, Fat 14.9 g, Protein 46.1 g

Ingredients:

4 Tilapia Fillets

⅔ cup sliced Almonds

1 cup Water

2 tbsp Dijon Mustard

1 tsp Olive Oil

¼ tsp Black Pepper

Directions:

1. Pour the water in your Power Pressure Cooker XL.
2. Mix the olive oil, pepper, and mustard in a small bowl.
3. Brush the fish fillets with the mustardy mixture on all sides.
4. Coat the fish in almonds slices.
5. Place the rack in your Power Pressure Cooker XL and arrange the fish fillets on it.
6. Close the lid and cook for 5 minutes on HIGH pressure.
7. Do a quick pressure release.

Shrimp and Egg Risotto

Serves: 6 \ Ready in: 30 minutes

Nutritional Info:

Calories 221, Carbohydrates 22 g, Fiber 1 g, Fat 10 g, Protein 13 g

Ingredients:

4 cups of Water

4 Garlic Cloves, minced

2 Eggs, beaten

½ tsp grated Ginger

3 tbsp Sesame Oil

¼ tsp Cayenne Pepper

1 ½ cups frozen Peas

2 cups Brown Rice

¼ cup Soy Sauce

1 cup chopped Onion

12 ounces peeled and pre-cooked Shrimp, thawed

Directions:

1. Heat some of the olive oil in your Power Pressure Cooker XL.
2. Scramble the eggs and transfer to a plate.
3. Heat the remaining oil and cook the onions and garlic for a minute or two.
4. Stir in the remaining ingredients except the shrimp and eggs.
5. Close the lid and cook on CHICKEN/MEAT for 18 minutes.
6. Wait about 10 minutes before doing a quick release. Stir in the shrimp and eggs.
7. And let them heat for a couple of seconds with the lid off.

Lobster and Gruyere Pasta

Serves: 4 \ Ready in: 15 minutes

Nutritional Info:

Calories 441, Carbohydrates 44 g, Fiber 0 g, Fat 15 g, Protein 28 g

Ingredients:

6 cups Water

1 tbsp Flour

8 ounces dried Ziti

1 cup Half & Half

1 tbsp chopped Tarragon

¾ cup Gruyere Cheese

3 Lobster Tails (about 6 ounces each)

½ cup White Wine

½ tsp Pepper

1 tbsp Worcestershire Sauce

Directions:

1. Add the water in the Power Pressure Cooker XL.
2. Add the lobster tails and ziti.
3. Close the lid and cook for 10 minutes on CHICKEN/MEAT.
4. Do a quick pressure release.
5. Drain the pasta and set aside.
6. Remove the meat from the tails, chop it, and stir into the bowl with pasta.
7. Stir in the rest of the ingredients in the Power Pressure Cooker XL.
8. When the sauce thickens add the pasta and lobster.
9. Cook for a minute or so.

Mediterranean Salmon

Serves: 4 \ Ready in: 15 minutes

Nutritional Info:

Calories 475.6 Carbohydrates 6.3 g, Fiber 2.7 g, Fat 31.5 g, Protein 42.9 g

Ingredients:

4 frozen Salmon Fillets

2 tbsp Olive Oil

1 Rosemary Sprig

1 cup Cherry Tomatoes

15 ounces Asparagus

1 cup Water

Directions:

1. Pour the water in your Power Pressure Cooker XL and insert the rack.
2. Place the salmon on the rack, top with rosemary, and arrange the asparagus on top. Close the lid and cook on HIGH for a minute and a half.
3. Add the cherry tomatoes on top and cook for 1 ½ to 2 more minutes.
4. Serve drizzled with olive oil.

Tuna and Pea Cheesy Noodles

Serves: 4 \ Ready in: 17 minutes

Nutritional Info:

Calories 430, Carbohydrates 42 g, Fiber 2 g, Fat 22 g, Protein 18 g

Ingredients:

1 can Tuna, drained

3 cups Water

4 ounces Cheddar Cheese, grated

16 ounces Egg Noodles

¼ cup Breadcrumbs

1 cup Frozen Peas

28 ounces canned Mushroom Soup

Directions:

1. Place the water and noodles in your Power Pressure Cooker XL.
2. Stir in soup, tuna, and frozen peas.
3. Close the lid and cook for 5 minutes on CHICKEN/MEAT.
4. Release the pressure quickly.
5. Stir in the cheese.
6. Transfer to a baking dish that can fit in your Power Pressure Cooker XL.
7. Sprinkle with breadcrumbs on top.
8. Place the baking dish in your Power Pressure Cooker XL, close the lid, and cook for a minute on HIGH pressure.

Scallops and Mussels Cauliflower Paella

Serves: 4 \ Ready in: 15 minutes

Nutritional Info:

Calories 154.6, Carbohydrates 11.3 g, Fiber 3.7 g, Fat 4.5 g, Protein 7.1 g

Ingredients:

2 Bell Peppers, diced

1 tbsp Coconut Oil

1 cup of Scallops

2 cups Mussels

1 Onion, diced

2 cups ground Cauliflower

2 cups Fish Stock

A pinch of Saffron

Directions:

1. Melt the coconut oil in your Power Pressure Cooker XL.

2. Add onions and bell peppers and cook for about 4 minutes.

3. Stir in scallops and saffron and cook for 2 minutes.

4. Stir in the remaining ingredients and close the lid.

5. Cook for 6 minutes on HIGH pressure.

Wrapped Fish and Potatoes

Serves: 4 \ Ready in: 15 minutes

Nutritional Info:

Calories 310, Carbohydrates 9 g, Fiber 3 g, Fat 14 g, Protein 30 g

Ingredients:

4 Fish Fillets (I used Salmon)

4 Thyme Sprigs

2 Medium Potatoes, sliced

1 Lemon, sliced thinly

1 Onion, sliced

A Handful of Fresh Parsley

2 cups of Water

2 tbsp Olive Oil

Directions:

1. Place each fish fillet onto a parchment paper. Divide the potatoes, thyme, parsley, onion, and lemon between the 4 parchment papers.

2. Drizzle each of them with ½ tbsp of olive oil and mix with your hands to coat everything.

3. Wrap the fish with the parchment paper.

4. Wrap each of the 'packets' in aluminum foil.

5. Pour the water in your Power Pressure Cooker XL.

6. Place the packets inside. If you are using a 6-quart Power Pressure Cooker XL you may need to cook 2 packets at a time.

7. Close the lid and cook for about 5 minutes on HIGH pressure.

Lemon Sauce Salmon

Serves: 4 \ Ready in: 10 minutes

Nutritional Info:

Calories 493, Carbohydrates 6.3 g, Fiber 0.3 g, Fat 31.5 g, Protein 41.2 g

Ingredients:

4 Salmon Fillets

1 tbsp Honey

½ tsp Cumin

1 tbsp Hot Water

1 tbsp Olive Oil

1 tsp Smoked Paprika

1 tbsp chopped Fresh Parsley

¼ cup Lemon Juice

1 cup of Water

Directions:

1. Pour the water inside your Power Pressure Cooker XL.

2. Place the salmon fillets on the rack.

3. Close the lid and cook for about 3 minutes on HIGH pressure.

4. Whisk together the remaining ingredients.

5. Release the pressure quickly, drizzle the sauce over the salmon.

6. Close the lid and cook for 2 more minutes.

Creamy Crabmeat

Serves: 4 \ Ready in: 12 minutes

Nutritional Info:

Calories 450, Carbohydrates 12.5 g, Fiber 0.3 g, Fat 10.4 g, Protein 40 g

Ingredients:

¼ cup Butter

1 small Red Onion, chopped

1 pound Lump Crabmeat

½ Celery Stalk, chopped

½ cup Heavy Cream

¼ cup Chicken Broth

Salt and Pepper, to taste

Directions:

1. Season the crabmeat with some salt and pepper to taste.

2. Melt the butter in your Power Pressure Cooker XL.

3. Add celery and cook for a minute.

4. Add onions and cook for 3 more minutes, or until soft.

5. Add the crabmeat and stir in the broth.

6. Close the lid and cook for 3 minutes on HIGH pressure.

7. Stir in the cream.

8. Season with some extra salt and pepper if needed.

Cod in a Tomato Sauce

Serves: 4 \ Ready in: 15 minutes

Nutritional Info:

Calories 251, Carbohydrates 3 g, Fiber 1 g, Fat 5.2 g, Protein 44.8 g

Ingredients:

4 Cod Fillets (about 7-ounce each)

2 cups chopped Tomatoes

1 cup of Water

1 tbsp Olive Oil

Salt and Pepper, to taste

¼ tsp Garlic Powder

Directions:

1. Place the tomatoes in a baking dish and crush them with a fork.
2. Season with some salt, pepper, and garlic powder.
3. Season the cod with salt and pepper and place it over the tomatoes.
4. Drizzle the olive oil over the fish and tomatoes.
5. Place the dish in your Power Pressure Cooker XL.
6. Close the lid and cook on HIGH pressure for 5 minutes.
7. Release the pressure naturally.

VEGETARIAN RECIPES

Meatless Shepherd's Pie

Serves: 4 \ Ready in: 17 minutes

Nutritional Info:

Calories 224.4, Carbohydrates 5.8 g, Fiber 0.1 g, Fat 14.6 g, Protein 15.6 g

Ingredients:

⅓ cup diced Celery

1 cup diced Onion

2 cups steamed and mashed Cauliflower

1 tbsp Olive Oil

½ cup diced Turnip

1 ¾ cup Veggie Broth

1 cup diced Tomatoes

1 cup grated Potatoes

½ cup diced Carrot

½ cup Water

Directions:

1. Heat the olive oil in your Power Pressure Cooker XL. Add onions, carrots, and celery, and cook for 3 minutes.

2. Stir in turnips, potatoes, and veggie broth. Close the lid and cook for 10 minutes on HIGH pressure. Stir in tomatoes.

3. Transfer the mixture to 4 ramekins. Top each ramekin with ½ cup of mashed cauliflower.

4. Pour the water inside your Power Pressure Cooker XL and place the trivet inside.

5. Close the lid and cook for 5 minutes on HIGH.

Vegetarian Spaghetti Bolognese

Serves: 8 \ Ready in: 25 minutes

Nutritional Info:

Calories 360, Carbohydrates 75 g, Fiber 8.2 g, Fat 2.3 g, Protein 15.1 g

Ingredients:

8 cups cooked Spaghetti

1 cup Cauliflower Florets

2 cups Shredded carrots

6 Garlic Cloves, minced

2 tbsp Tomato Paste

2 tbsp Agave Nectar

1 ½ tbsp dried Oregano

56 ounces canned crushed Tomatoes

2 tbsp Balsamic Vinegar

1 tbsp dried Basil

10 ounces Mushrooms

2 cups chopped Eggplant

1 cup Water

1 ½ tsp dried Rosemary

Salt and Black Pepper, to taste

Directions:

1. Add cauliflower, mushrooms, eggplant, and carrots to a food processor and process until finely ground.

2. Add them to your Power Pressure Cooker XL. Stir in the rest of the ingredients.

3. Close the lid and cook for 8 minutes on CHICKEN/MEAT. Release the pressure naturally. Serve the sauce over spaghetti.

Pressure Cooked Ratatouille

Serves: 4 \ Ready in: 20 minutes

Nutritional Info:

Calories 104, Carbohydrates 10.4 g, Fiber 0.5 g, Fat 7.2 g, Protein 1.5 g

Ingredients:

1 Zucchini, sliced

2 Tomatoes, sliced

1 tbsp Balsamic Vinegar

1 Eggplant, sliced

1 Onion, sliced

1 tbsp dried Thyme

2 tbsp Olive Oil

2 Garlic Cloves, minced

1 cup Water

Directions:

1. Add the garlic in a springform pan.
2. Arrange the veggies in a circle.
3. Sprinkle them with thyme and drizzle with olive oil.
4. Pour the water in your Power Pressure Cooker XL.
5. Place the pan inside.
6. Close the lid and cook for 6 minutes on HIGH pressure.
7. Release the pressure naturally.

Bean and Rice Casserole

Serves: 4 \ Ready in: 25 minutes

Nutritional Info:

Calories 322, Carbohydrates 63 g, Fiber 9 g, Fat 2 g, Protein 6 g

Ingredients:

1 cup soaked Black Beans

5 cups Water

2 tsp Onion Powder

2 tsp Chili Powder, optional

2 cups Brown Rice

6 ounces Tomato Paste

1 tsp minced Garlic

1 tsp Salt

Directions:

1. Combine all of the ingredients in your Power Pressure Cooker XL.
2. Choose the CHICKEN/MEAT setting and close the lid. Cook for 25 minutes. Release the pressure quickly.

Potato Chili

Serves: 4 \ Ready in: 30 minutes

Nutritional Info:

Calories 297, Carbohydrates 53 g, Fiber 35 g, Fat 4 g, Protein 16 g

Ingredients:

15 ounces canned Black Beans, rinsed and drained

2 cups Veggie Broth

28 ounces canned diced Tomatoes

15 ounces canned Kidney Beans, rinsed and drained

1 Sweet Potato, chopped

1 Red Onion, chopped

1 Red Bell Pepper, chopped

1 Green Bell Pepper, chopped

1 tbsp Olive Oil

1 tbsp Chili Powder

¼ tsp Cinnamon

1 tsp Cumin

2 tsp Cocoa Powder

1 tsp Cayenne

Pepper Salt, to taste

Directions:

1. Heat the olive oil in your Power Pressure Cooker XL. Add onions, peppers, and potatoes.
2. Cook until the onions become translucent. Stir in the rest of the ingredients.
3. Close the lid and cook on CHICKEN/MEAT for 12 minutes. Release the pressure naturally.

Veggie Burger Patties

Serves: 4 \ Ready in: 20 minutes

Nutritional Info:

Calories 221, Carbohydrates 34.3 g, Fiber 6.5 g, Fat 7.1 g, Protein 3.4 g

Ingredients:

1 Zucchini, peeled and grated

3 cups Cauliflower Florets

1 Carrot, grated

⅔ cup Veggie Broth

2 cups Broccoli Florets

½ Onion, diced

½ tsp Turmeric Powder

2 tbsp Olive Oil

2 cups Sweet Potato cubes

¼ tsp Black Pepper

Directions:

1. Heat one tbsp oil in your Power Pressure Cooker XL. Sauté the onions for about 3 minutes.
2. Add the carrots and cook for an additional minute. Add potatoes and broth.
3. Close the lid and cook on CHICKEN/MEAT for 10 minutes.
4. Release the pressure quickly. Stir in the remaining veggies.
5. Close the lid and cook for 3 minutes on HIGH pressure.
6. Mash the veggies with a masher and stir in the seasonings.
7. Let cool for a few minutes and make burger patties out of the mixture.
8. Heat the rest of the oil. Cook the patties for about a minute on each side.

Fake Mushroom Risotto the Paleo Way

Serves: 4 \ Ready in: 30 minutes

Nutritional Info:

Calories 117.2, Carbohydrates 13.4 g, Fiber 5.5 g, Fat 11.1 g, Protein 2.8 g

Ingredients:

1 ½ head Cauliflower

2 cups sliced Mushrooms

1 Garlic Clove, minced

1 tsp dried Basil

1 Carrot, grated

1 cup Veggie Broth

1 tbsp Olive Oil

½ Onion, diced

Directions:

1. Cut the cauliflower into pieces and place them in your food processor.
2. Process until really ground (cauliflower rice). You should have about 6 cups of cauliflower rice.
3. Heat the oil in your Power Pressure Cooker XL. Sauté the carrots and onions for 3 minutes.
4. Add the garlic and cook for one more minute. Stir in all of the remaining ingredients.
5. Close the lid and let cook for 5 minutes on HIGH pressure.
6. Do a quick pressure release.

Spicy Moong Beans

Serves: 8 \ Ready in: 30 minutes

Nutritional Info:

Calories 328, Carbohydrates 62.4 g, Fiber 8.3 g, Fat 4.8 g, Protein 9.6 g

Ingredients:

1 tsp Paprika

2 tsp Curry Powder

4 cups Moong Beans, soaked and drained

1 Onion, diced

1 tsp Turmeric

Juice of 1 Lime

1 Jalapeno Pepper, chopped

1 Sprig Curry Leaves

4 Garlic Cloves, minced

2 tbsp Olive Oil

1 ½ tsp Cumin Seeds

2 Tomatoes, chopped

Salt, to taste

1-inch piece of Ginger, grated

Directions:

1. Heat the oil in your Power Pressure Cooker XL.Add the cumin seeds and cook for about a minute and a half. Add onion and cook until translucent.

2. Add garlic along with curry, turmeric, ginger, and some salt. Cook for one more minute.

3. Stir in jalapeno, and tomatoes and cook for 5 minutes, or until soft.

4. Add the beans and pour water to cover the ingredients. Cover by at least 2 inches.

5. Add the lime juice and curry leaves and close the lid.

6. Cook for 15 minutes on HIGH pressure. Release the pressure naturally.

Tamari Tofu with Sweet Potatoes and Broccoli

Serves: 4 \ Ready in: 15 minutes

Nutritional Info:

Calories 250, Carbohydrates 22 g, Fiber 2 g, Fat 12 g, Protein 17 g

Ingredients:

1 pound Tofu, cubed

3 Garlic Cloves, minced

2 tbsp Tamari

2 tbsp Sesame Seeds

2 tsp toasted Sesame Oil

2 tbsp Tahini

1 tbsp Rice Vinegar

⅓ cup Vegetable Stock

2 cups Onion slices

2 cups Broccoli Florets

1 cup diced Sweet Potato

2 tbsp Sriracha

Directions:

1. Heat the sesame oil in your Power Pressure Cooker XL.
2. Add onion and sweet potatoes and cook for 2 minutes.
3. Add garlic and half of the sesame seeds, and cook for a minute.
4. Stir in tamari, broth, tofu, and vinegar.
5. Close the lid and cook for 3 minutes on CHICKEN/MEAT.
6. Release the pressure quickly, add broccoli, and close the lid again. Cook for 2 more minutes. Stir in sriracha and tahini before serving.

Tomato Zoodles

Serves: 4 \ Ready in: 20 minutes

Nutritional Info:

Calories 71.7, Carbohydrates 9.6 g, Fiber 2.5 g, Fat 3.8 g, Protein 1.9 g

Ingredients:

4 cups Zoodles

2 Garlic Cloves, minced

8 cups Boiling Water

1 tbsp Olive Oil

½ cup Tomato Paste

2 cups canned diced Tomatoes

2 tbsp chopped Basil

Directions:

1. Place the zoodles in a bowl filled with boiling water.

2. After one minute, drain them and set aside.

3. Heat the oil in your Power Pressure Cooker XL. Add garlic and cook for about a minute, just until fragrant.

4. Add tomato paste and basil.

5. Stir in the zoodles, coating them well with the sauce.

6. Close the lid and cook on CHICKEN/MEAT for one minute.

7. Release the pressure quickly.

Sweet Potato and Baby Carrot Medley

Serves: 4 \ Ready in: 30 minutes

Nutritional Info:

Calories 412.9, Carbohydrates 81.3 g, Fiber 13 g, Fat 7.5 g, Protein 7 g

Ingredients:

1 tsp dried Oregano

2 tbsp Olive Oil

½ cup Veggie Broth

1 Onion, finely chopped

2 pounds Sweet Potatoes, cubed

2 pounds Baby Carrots, halved

Directions:

1. Heat the olive oil in your pressure cooker.
2. Add onions and cook for 3 minutes.
3. Add the carrots and cook for 3 more minutes.
4. Add potatoes, carrots, broth, and oregano.
5. Close the lid and cook for about 8 minutes on HIGH pressure.

Leafy Green Risotto

Serves: 6 \ Ready in: 20 minutes

Nutritional Info:

Calories 272, Carbohydrates 40 g, Fiber 3 g, Fat 11 g, Protein 6 g

Ingredients:

3 ½ cups Veggie Broth

1 cup Spinach Leaves, packed

1 cup Kale Leaves, packed

¼ cup grated Parmesan Cheese

¼ cup diced Onion

3 tbsp Butter

2 tsp Olive Oil

1 ½ cups Arborio Rice

4 Sun-dried Tomatoes, chopped

Pinch of Nutmeg

Salt and Pepper, to taste

Directions:

1. Heat the olive oil in your cooker.
2. Add onions and cook until soft.

3. Add rice and cook for 3-4 minutes.

4. Pour the broth over.

5. Close the lid and cook for 6 minutes on "Rice/Risotto" mode.

6. Do a quick pressure release and stir in the remaining ingredients.

7. Leave for a minute or two or until the greens become wilted.

APPETIZERS RECIPES

Thyme-Flavored Fries

Serves: 4 \ Ready in: 13 minutes

Nutritional Info:

Calories 116, Carbohydrates 24.4 g, Fiber 3 g, Fat 1.4 g, Protein 1.8 g

Ingredients:

1 pound Potatoes, cut into strips

1 tbsp dried Thyme

½ tsp Garlic Powder

1 tsp Olive Oil

1 cup Water

Directions:

1. Place the potatoes in a large bowl. Add thyme, olive oil, and garlic, and mix to coat them well. Pour the water into your Power Pressure Cooker XL.

2. Arrange the fries in a veggie steamer in a single layer. Close the lid and cook for 3 minutes on HIGH pressure. Do a quick pressure release.

Buttery Parsley Corn

Serves: 4 \ Ready in: 10 minutes

Nutritional Info:

Calories 310, Carbohydrates 32 g, Fiber 12 g, Fat 21 g, Protein 5 g

Ingredients:

4 ears shucked Corn

6 tbsp Butter

½ tsp Salt

1 ⅓ cups Water

½ tsp Chili Powder, optional

¼ tsp Sugar

2 tbsp minced Parsley

Directions:

1. Combine the water, salt, sugar, and chili powder if using, in your pressure cooker.
2. Heat 2 tbsp butter and add the corn.
3. Close the lid and cook on CHICKEN/MEAT for 3 minutes.
4. Release the pressure quickly and set the corn aside.
5. Heat the remaining butter and add parsley.
6. When fully melted, pour the parsley butter over the corn.

Kale Chips with Garlic and Lime Juice

Serves: 4 \ Ready in: 15 minutes

Nutritional Info:

Calories 66.5, Carbohydrates 7.7 g, Fiber 2.4 g, Fat 3.8 g, Protein 2.3 g

Ingredients:

1 pound Kale

½ cup Water

3 Garlic Cloves, minced

1 tbsp Olive Oil

2 tbsp Lime Juice

Directions:

1. Wash the kale and remove the stems.
2. Heat the oil in your Power Pressure Cooker XL.

3. Add garlic and cook for a minute, or just until fragrant.

4. Pack the kale well inside the cooker.

5. Close the lid and cook for 5 minutes on HIGH pressure.

6. Do a quick pressure release. Transfer to a bowl. Drizzle the lime juice over.

Creamy Potato Slices with Chives

Serves: 6 \ Ready in: 15 minutes

Nutritional Info:

Calories 168, Carbohydrates 31 g, Fiber 3 g, Fat 3 g, Protein 4 g

Ingredients:

6 Potatoes

⅓ cup Sour Cream

2 tbsp Potato Starch

1 tbsp chopped Chives

⅓ cup Milk

1 cup Chicken Broth

1 tsp Salt

Pinch of Pepper

Directions:

1. Peel and slice the potatoes. Coat them with salt, chives, and pepper.

2. Add broth and potatoes in your Power Pressure Cooker XL.

3. Cook for about 3 minutes on HIGH pressure.

4. Release the pressure quickly. Transfer to a bowl.

5. Whisk the remaining ingredients into the cooking liquid in your Power Pressure Cooker XL. Cook for one minute while whisking constantly.

6. Pour the sauce over the potatoes.

Hummus Under Pressure

Serves: 8 \ Ready in: 20 minutes

Nutritional Info:

Calories 161, Carbohydrates 20.2 g, Fiber 5.9 g, Fat 6.4 g, Protein 8 g

Ingredients:

1 Onion, quartered

1 Bay Leaf

2 tbsp Soy Sauce

¼ cup Tahini

¾ cup Garbanzo Beans

¼ cup dried Soybeans

¼ cup chopped Parsley

1 cup Veggie Broth

Juice of 1 Lemon

2 Garlic Cloves, minced

Directions:

1. Add garbanzo beans, soybeans, and broth in your Power Pressure Cooker XL.
2. Pour some water over to cover them by one inch.
3. Close the lid and cook for 15 minutes on HIGH pressure.
4. Release the pressure naturally.
5. Drain the beans and save the cooking liquid.
6. Place the beans along with the remaining ingredients into a food processor.
7. Proccss until smooth.
8. Add some of the cooking liquid to make the hummus thinner, if you want to.

Barbecue Wings

Serves: 4 \ Ready in: 15 minutes

Nutritional Info:

Calories 140.7, Carbohydrates 2 g, Fiber 0.2 g, Fat 3.3 g, Protein 19.5 g

Ingredients:

12 Chicken Wings

¼ cup Barbecue Sauce

1 cup of Water

Directions:

1. Place the chicken wings and water in your Power Pressure Cooker XL.
2. Close the lid and cook for 5 minutes on HIGH pressure.
3. Release the pressure quickly.
4. Rinse under cold water and pat the wings dry.
5. Place them in your Power Pressure Cooker XL and pour the barbecue sauce over.
6. Mix with your hands to coat them well.
7. Close the lid and cook with the lid off on all sides, until sticky.

Mini Mac and Cheese

Serves: 4 \ Ready in: 17 minutes

Nutritional Info:

Calories 132, Carbohydrates 15.4 g, Fiber 1.6 g, Fat 5.4 g, Protein 7 g

Ingredients:

8 ounces whole-wheat Macaroni

¾ cup shredded Monterey Jack Cheese

2 cups Water

Directions:

1. Place the macaroni and water in your Power Pressure Cooker XL.
2. Choose the "rice" setting and cook for 5 minutes.
3. Drain the macaroni and place them back in the pressure cooker,
4. Stir in the Monterey cheese and cook for 30 seconds until really well melted.
5. Divide between 4 small bowls.

Asparagus Dressed in Bacon

Serves: 4 \ Ready in: 17 minutes

Nutritional Info:

Calories 224.4, Carbohydrates 5.8 g, Fiber 0.1 g, Fat 14.6 g, Protein 15.6 g

Ingredients:

1 pound of Asparagus

8 ounces of Bacon

1 cup of Water

Directions:

1. Pour the water into your pressure cooker. Cut off the ends of the asparagus.
2. Slice the bacon in enough strips to cover each asparagus spear.
3. Wrap the asparagus in bacon.
4. Arrange the wrapped asparagus on a steamer basket.
5. Place the basket inside the Power Pressure Cooker XL.
6. Close the lid and cook for 4 minutes on CHICKEN/MEAT.
7. Release the pressure quickly.

Lemony and Garlicky Potato and Turnip Dip

Serves: 4 \ Ready in: 15 minutes

Nutritional Info:

Calories 143.5, Carbohydrates 12.3 g, Fiber 1.7 g, Fat 10.4 g, Protein 1.2 g

Ingredients:

3 tbsp Olive Oil

6 Whole Garlic Cloves, peeled

2 tbsp Lemon Juice

1 Turnip, cut lengthwise

1 Sweet Potato, cut lengthwise

1 cup Water

2 tbsp Coconut Milk

Directions:

1. Pour the water into your Power Pressure Cooker XL. Place the potato, turnip, and garlic on the rack. Close the lid and cook for 10 minutes on HIGH pressure.

2. Place the veggies in a food processor and add the remaining ingredients.

3. Process until smooth. Transfer to a container with a lid. Refrigerate before serving.

Pressure Cooked Devilled Eggs

Serves: 4 \ Ready in: 15 minutes

Nutritional Info:

Calories 100, Carbohydrates 0.7 g, Fiber 0.2 g, Fat 7.9 g, Protein 6.4 g

Ingredients:

4 Eggs

1 tsp Paprika

1 tbsp light Mayonnaise

1 cup of Water

Directions:

1. Place the eggs and water in your Power Pressure Cooker XL.

2. Close the lid and cook for 5 minutes on HIGH pressure. Let the pressure release naturally. Place the eggs in an ice bath and let cool for 5 minutes.

3. Peel and cut them in half. Whisk together the remaining ingredients. Top the egg halves with the mixture.

Easy Street Sweet Corn

Serves: 6 \ Ready in: 5 minutes

Nutritional Info:

Calories 130, Carbohydrates 16 g, Fiber 2.4 g, Fat 5 g, Protein 9 g

Ingredients:

Juice of 2 Limes

1 cup grated Parmesan Cheese

6 Ears Sweet Corn

2 cups Water

6 tbsp Yogurt

½ tsp Garlic Powder

Directions:

1. Pour the water into your Power Pressure Cooker XL. Place the corn in a steamer basket and inside the Power Pressure Cooker XL. Close the lid and cook for 3 minutes on HIGH pressure.

2. Combine the remaining ingredients, except the cheese, in a bowl. Release the pressure quickly and let cool for a couple of minutes.

3. Remove the husks from the corn and brush them with the mixture. Sprinkle the parmesan on top.

DESSERT RECIPES

Full Coconut Cake

Serves: 4 \ Ready in: 55 minutes

Nutritional Info:

Calories 350, Carbohydrates 47 g, Fiber 7.5 g, Fat 14.1 g, Protein 7.5 g

Ingredients:

3 Eggs, yolks and whites separated

¾ cup Coconut Flour

½ tsp Coconut Extract

1 ½ cups warm Coconut Milk

½ cup Coconut Sugar

2 tbsp melted Coconut Oil

1 cup Water

Directions:

1. Beat the whites until soft form peaks. Beat in the egg yolks along with the coconut sugar.
2. Stir in coconut extract and coconut oil.
3. Gently fold in the coconut flour. Line a baking dish and pour the batter inside. Cover with aluminum foil.
4. Pour the water inside your Power Pressure Cooker XL.
5. Place the dish in the pressure cooker.
6. Close the lid and cook for 40 minutes on HIGH.
7. Do a quick pressure release.

Compote with Blueberries and Lemon Juice

Serves: 4 \ Ready in: 10 minutes

Nutritional Info:

Calories 220, Carbohydrates 61.2 g, Fiber 3.9 g, Fat 0.3 g, Protein 1.2 g

Ingredients:

2 cups Frozen Blueberries

2 tbsp Arrowroot or Cornstarch

¾ cups Coconut Sugar

Juice of ½ Lemon

2 tbsp Water

Directions:

1. Place blueberries, lemon juice, and sugar in your Power Pressure Cooker XL.
2. Close the lid and cook for 3 minutes on HIGH pressure.
3. Release the pressure naturally for 10 minutes. Meanwhile, combine the arrowroot and water.
4. Stir the mixture into the cooked blueberries and cook until the mixture thickens.
5. Transfer the compote to a bowl and let cool completely. Refrigerate before serving.

Oatmeal Chocolate Cookies

Serves: 2 \ Ready in: 30 minutes

Nutritional Info:

Calories 412, Carbohydrates 59 g, Fiber 1 g, Fat 20 g, Protein 6 g

Ingredients:

¼ cup Whole Wheat Flour

¼ cup Oats

1 tbsp Butter

2 tbsp Sugar

½ tsp Vanilla Extract

1 tbsp Honey

2 tbsp Milk

2 tsp Coconut Oil

1/8 tsp Sea Salt

3 tbsp Chocolate Chips

Directions:

1. Combine all of the ingredients in a large bowl.
2. Line a baking pan with parchment paper.
3. Make lemon-sized cookies out of the mixture and flatten them onto the lined pan.
4. Add some water in your Power Pressure Cooker XL and lower the trivet.
5. Add the baking pan inside your Power Pressure Cooker XL.
6. Cook for about 15 minutes. The CHICKEN/MEAT setting will cook them to perfection. Release the pressure quickly.

Peanut Butter Bars

Serves: 6 \ Ready in: 30 minutes

Nutritional Info:

Calories 561, Carbohydrates 61 g, Fiber 1.50 g, Fat 18 g, Protein 8 g

Ingredients:

1 cup Flour

1 ½ cups Water

1 Egg

⅓ cup powdered Peanut Butter

⅓ cup Peanut Butter, softened

½ cup Butter, softened

1 cup Oats

½ cup Sugar

½ tsp Baking Soda

½ tsp Salt

½ cup Brown Sugar

Directions:

1. Grease a springform pan and line it with parchment paper.
2. Beat together the eggs, powdered peanut butter, softened peanut butter, butter, salt, white sugar, and brown sugar.
3. Fold in the oats, flour, and baking soda. Press the batter into the pan.
4. Cover the pan with a paper towel and then with a piece of aluminum foil.
5. Pour the water into the pressure cooker and lower the trivet.
6. Place the pan inside and close the lid. Cook for 20 minutes on CHICKEN/MEAT. Release the pressure naturally.
7. Wait for about 10 minutes before inverting onto a plate and cutting into bars.

Poached Pears with Orange and Ginger

Serves: 4 \ Ready in: 12 minutes

Nutritional Info:

Calories 170.4, Carbohydrates 43.7 g, Fiber 5.2 g, Fat 0.6 g, Protein 1.1 g

Ingredients:

4 Pears cut in half

1 tsp powdered Ginger

1 tsp Nutmeg

1 cup Orange Juice

2 tsp Cinnamon

⅓ cup Coconut Sugar

Directions:

1. Combine the juice and spices in your Power Pressure Cooker XL.
2. Place the pears on the trivet. Close the lid and cook for 7 minutes on HIGH pressure.
3. Release the pressure after 5 minutes. Place the pears onto a serving plate.
4. Pour the juice over.

Milk Dumplings in Sweet Cardamom Sauce

Serves: 20 \ Ready in: 25 minutes

Nutritional Info:

Calories 134, Carbohydrates 28.7 g, Fiber 0 g, Fat 1.5 g, Protein 2.4 g

Ingredients:

6 cups Water

2 ½ cups Sugar

3 tbsp Lime Juice

6 cups Milk

1 tsp ground Cardamom

Directions:

1. Place the milk in a pot inside your Power Pressure Cooker XL (or you can do this on the stove if you prefer) and bring it to a boil. Stir in the lime juice. The solids should start to separate.
2. Pour the milk through a cheesecloth-lined colander.

3. Drain as much liquid as you possibly can.

4. Place the paneer on a smooth surface.

5. Form a ball and then divide it into 20 equal pieces.

6. Pour the water in your pressure cooker and bring it to a boil.

7. Add sugar and cardamom and cook until dissolved.

8. Shape the dumplings into balls, and place them in the syrup.

9. Close the lid and cook on CHICKEN/MEAT for 5 minutes.

10. Let cool and then refrigerate until Ready to serve.

Pressure Cooked Cherry Pie

Serves: 6 \ Ready in: 20 minutes

Nutritional Info:

Calories 393, Carbohydrates 70.6 g, Fiber 1.6 g, Fat 12 g, Protein 2 g

Ingredients:

1 9-inch double Pie Crust

2 cups Water

½ tsp Vanilla Extract

4 cups Cherries, pitted

¼ tsp Almond Extract

4 tbsp Quick Tapioca

1 cup Sugar

A pinch of Salt

Directions:

1. Pour the water inside your Power Pressure Cooker XL and lower the trivet.

2. Combine the cherries with tapioca, sugar, extracts, and salt.

3. Place one pie crust on the bottom of a lined springform pan.

4. Spread the filling over. Top with the other crust. Place the pan inside the Power Pressure Cooker XL.

5. Close the lid and cook for 18 minutes on CHICKEN/MEAT.

6. Wait 10 minutes before releasing the pressure quickly.

Crème Caramel Coconut Flan

Serves: 4 \ Ready in: 30 minutes

Nutritional Info:

Calories 107.8, Carbohydrates 16.5 g, Fiber 0 g, Fat 3.3 g, Protein 3.3 g

Ingredients:

2 Eggs

7 ounces Condensed Coconut Milk

½ cups Coconut Milk

1 ½ cups Water

½ tsp Vanilla

Directions:

1. Place a pan with a heavy bottom in your Power Pressure Cooker XL.

2. Place the sugar in the pan.

3. Cook until a caramel is formed.

4. Divide the caramel between 4 small ramekins.

5. Pour the water in the pressure cooker and lower the trivet.

6. Beat the rest of the ingredients together and divide them between the ramekins.

7. Cover them with aluminum foil and place in the Power Pressure Cooker XL.

8. Close the lid and cook for 5 minutes on CHICKEN/MEAT. Release the pressure naturally.

Lemon and Chocolate Bread Pudding

Serves: 4 \ Ready in: 25 minutes

Nutritional Info:

Calories 467, Carbohydrates 51 g, Fiber 1 g, Fat 14 g, Protein 12 g

Ingredients:

3 ½ cups cubed Bread

¾ cup Heavy Cream

1 tsp Butter

2 tbsp Lemon Juice

Zest of 1 Lemon

3 Eggs

3 ounces Chocolate, chopped

½ cup Milk

⅓ cup plus 1 tbsp Sugar

2 cups Water

1 tsp Almond Extract Pinch of Salt

Directions:

1. Pour the water in your Power Pressure Cooker XL. Grease a baking dish with butter.

2. Beat the eggs along with 1/3 cup sugar. Stir in cream, lemon juice, zest, extract, milk, and salt. Soak the bread for 5 minutes.

3. Stir in the chocolate. Pour the batter into the dish. Sprinkle the remaining sugar on top.

4. Close the lid and cook for 18 minutes on CHICKEN/MEAT.

5. Release the pressure naturally.

Easiest Pressure Cooked Raspberry Curd

Serves: 5 \ Ready in: 25 minutes

Nutritional Info:

Calories 249, Carbohydrates 48.4 g, Fiber 4.6 g, Fat 6.8 g, Protein 1.8 g

Ingredients:

12 ounces Raspberries

2 tbsp Butter

Juice of ½ Lemon

1 cup Sugar

2 Egg Yolks

Directions:

1. Combine the raspberries, sugar, and lemon juice in your Power Pressure Cooker XL.
2. Close the lid and cook for a minute on HIGH pressure.
3. Release the pressure naturally for 5 minutes.
4. Puree the raspberries and discard the seeds.
5. Whisk the yolks in a bowl.
6. Combine the yolks with the hot raspberry puree.
7. Pour the mixture in your Power Pressure Cooker XL.
8. Cook with the lid off for a minute.
9. Stir in the butter and cook for a couple more minutes, until thick.
10. Transfer to a container with a lid.
11. Refrigerate before serving.

A Different Pumpkin Pie

Serves: 4 \ Ready in: 30 minutes

Nutritional Info:

Calories 172.2, Carbohydrates 39.4 g, Fiber 3.6 g, Fat 1.9 g, Protein 2.8 g

Ingredients:

1 pound Butternut Squash, diced

1 Egg

⅓ cup Honey

½ cup Milk, preferably Coconut

½ tsp Cinnamon

½ tbsp Arrowroot or Cornstarch

1 cup Water

Pinch of Sea Salt

Directions:

1. Place the water inside your Power Pressure Cooker XL. Place the butternut squash in the basket.
2. Close the lid and cook for 4 minutes on HIGH pressure.
3. Whisk all of the remaining ingredients in a bowl.
4. Drain the squash well and add it to the milk mixture.
5. Pour the batter into a greased baking dish. Place in the Power Pressure Cooker XL.
6. Close the lid and cook for 10 minutes on HIGH pressure.

CONCLUSION

Now that you have delicious and quick to make recipes for your Power Pressure Cooker XL, it is only a matter of time before you start creating amazing delicacies of your own.

I hope that this book was able to show you why the Power Pressure Cooker XL is a way better investment than any similar appliance on the market, and that you will deeply enjoy every single bite of these mouthwatering recipes found in this cookbook.

Throw away your pans and skillets, because the Power Pressure Cooker XL is about to become the only cooking tool you will ever need.

Danielle Jones